WILDERNESS
SURVIVAL SKILLS

FINDING FOOD
IN THE WILD

MOLLY MACK

PowerKiDS
press.

New York

Published in 2016 by The Rosen Publishing Group, Inc.
29 East 21st Street, New York, NY 10010

First Edition

Editor: Sarah Machajewski
Book Design: Michael J. Flynn

Photo Credits: Cover Jordon Siemens/Digital Vision/Getty Images; cover, pp. 1, 3–4, 6, 8, 10, 12, 14, 16, 18, 20, 22–24 (map background), 13 (dandelions) Sergei Drozd/Shutterstock.com; p. 5 Ari V/Shutterstock.com; p. 6 (book) belkos/Shutterstock.com; p. 6 (fruits) SusaZoom/Shutterstock.com; p. 7 Falcon Eyes/Shutterstock.com; p. 9 JupiterImages/Photolibrary/Getty Images; p. 10 Olha Rohulya/Shutterstock.com; p. 11 © iStockphoto.com/Maica; p. 12 Gabriele Maltinti/Shutterstock.com; p. 13 (background) exopixel/Shutterstock.com; p. 13 (cattails) GazTaechin/Shutterstock.com; p. 13 (clover) Laitr Keiows/Shutterstock.com; p. 13 (wild garlic) Carlos Amarillo/Shutterstock.com; p. 13 (wild onions) Jacqui Martin/Shutterstock.com; p. 13 (wild leeks) Foodpictures/Shutterstock.com; p. 13 (purslane) TwilightArtPictures/Shutterstock.com; p. 15 (poison hemlock) Aleksandr Stepanov/Shutterstock.com; p. 15 (Queen Anne's lace) Leslie Weisgerber/Shutterstock.com; p. 17 Philippe Henry/Oxford Scientific/Getty Images; p. 19 (anthropoid) Twenty20 Inc/Shutterstock.com; p. 19 (fried grasshoppers) Cahir Davitt/AWL Images/Getty Images; p. 20 Leonardo Patrizi/E+/Getty Images; p. 21 Blend Images/Shutterstock.com; p. 22 © iStockphoto.com/mediaphotos.

Cataloging-in-Publication Data

Mack, Molly.
Finding food in the wild / by Molly Mack.
p. cm. — (Wilderness survival skills)
Includes index.
ISBN 978-1-5081-4307-9 (pbk.)
ISBN 978-1-5081-4308-6 (6-pack)
ISBN 978-1-5081-4309-3 (library binding)
1. Wilderness survival — Juvenile literature. 2. Survival — Juvenile literature. 3. Survival skills — Juvenile literature. I. Mack, Molly. II. Title.
GV200.5 M28 2016
613.69—d23

Manufactured in the United States of America

CPSIA Compliance Information: Batch #BW16PK: For Further Information contact Rosen Publishing, New York, New York at 1-800-237-9932

CONTENTS

A NOTE TO READERS

Always talk with a parent or teacher before proceeding with any of the activities found in this book. Some activities require adult supervision.

A NOTE TO PARENTS AND TEACHERS

This book was written to be informative and entertaining. Some of the activities in this book require adult supervision. Please talk with your child or student before allowing them to proceed with any wilderness activities. The authors and publisher specifically disclaim any liability for injury or damages that may result from use of information in this book.

MAN VS. NATURE

Many people love spending time in the **wilderness**. Whether you camp, hike, or just enjoy being outside, spending time outdoors is a great way to get to know nature. However, many things in the wilderness can put your safety and survival at risk.

Knowing basic survival skills will help you be prepared for anything. Survival skills include making **shelter**, building fire, finding water, and more. This book will help you learn about finding food in the wilderness that's safe to eat. Let's get started!

SURVIVAL TIP
Finding food in the wilderness is also called foraging.

This boy prepared for his trip into the wilderness by packing food. However, it's also important to know how to find it.

5

BE PREPARED!

The most important survival skill is simple: be prepared! One way to prepare is to pack the right amount of food for the time you're spending in the wilderness. You don't want to run out before your trip is over. You also don't want to carry more than you need.

Knowing the conditions of where you're going will help you prepare. For example, if it's hot, don't bring food that will go bad or melt. If it's far away, don't pack anything too heavy to carry. Time spent preparing is time well spent!

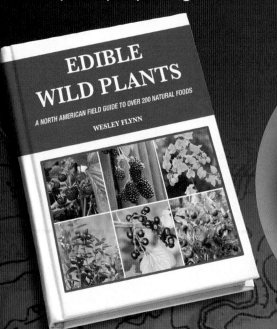

EDIBLE
WILD PLANTS
A NORTH AMERICAN FIELD GUIDE TO OVER 200 NATURAL FOODS
WESLEY FLYNN

SURVIVAL TIP

All wilderness lovers should have a plant **identification** guide. It has pictures and **descriptions** of safe and harmful plants. Look for one at your local library.

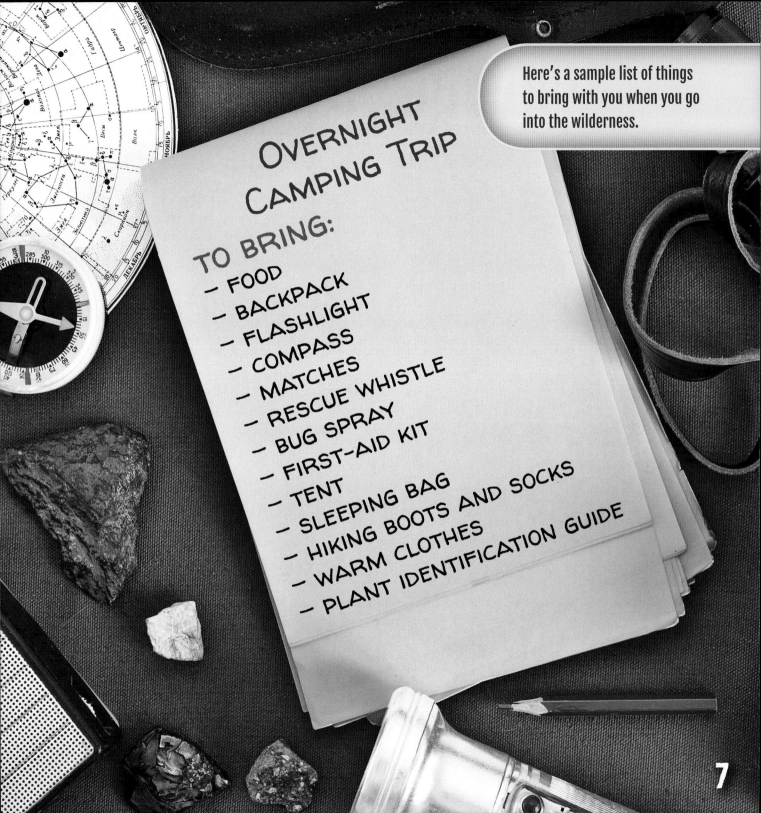

Overnight Camping Trip

TO BRING:
- FOOD
- BACKPACK
- FLASHLIGHT
- COMPASS
- MATCHES
- RESCUE WHISTLE
- BUG SPRAY
- FIRST-AID KIT
- TENT
- SLEEPING BAG
- HIKING BOOTS AND SOCKS
- WARM CLOTHES
- PLANT IDENTIFICATION GUIDE

Here's a sample list of things to bring with you when you go into the wilderness.

WHY DO WE EAT?

Food gives us **energy**. It powers our bodies so we can do fun activities like camp and hike. These activities use a lot of energy, though. Eating helps us **refuel**.

If you find yourself without food, don't panic. The human body can last several days without it. It will use stores of fat as energy when there's a lack of food. However, you never want to reach this point. It's important to keep your energy levels up so you can get into and out of the wilderness safely.

SURVIVAL TIP

If you're lost in the woods, first find water and a safe place to stay. Finding food can wait!

You're sure to get pretty hungry while you're being active outside. Bring snacks you can eat while you're hiking, climbing, or walking. Nuts, seeds, and energy bars are light and give you lots of energy.

EXPECTING THE UNEXPECTED

It's always important to prepare before heading outdoors. However, sometimes things happen you can't prepare for. Maybe you went camping, but your food was lost or stolen. Or maybe a wild animal ate what you packed.

You never know what might happen when you go into the wilderness. Luckily, there's plenty of food around you. The outdoors is full of food that can help you survive—as long as you know how to find it. This includes plants, animals, and bugs. Let's learn about some of them.

WILD BLUEBERRIES

Finding food in the wilderness is easy, but you must be careful. For every plant, animal, and bug you *can* eat, there are many you can't.

EDIBLE WILD PLANTS

Nature is made of wild plants. Some of them are edible. "Edible" means you can eat it. Read up on edible plants before you head outdoors—correct identification is the most important skill you can have.

What plants you'll find depends on where you are. However, common wild edible plants include clover, cattail, nettle, chicory, and purslane. Wild garlic, wild onions, and wild leeks are also safe to eat. You can identify them by their strong smell. Dandelions—familiar backyard plants—are entirely edible. You can eat their flowers, leaves, and roots!

SURVIVAL TIP

In ocean areas, kelp and seaweed are safe wild plants to eat.

COMMON EDIBLE PLANTS

These are just a few edible wild plants. Become familiar with how they look so you can spot them in nature.

DANDELION
FLOWER, LEAVES, ROOT

CATTAIL
ROOT, STEM, LEAVES, YOUNG FLOWER

CLOVER
FLOWER, LEAVES, ROOT

WILD GARLIC
LEAVES, STEM, ROOT

WILD ONIONS
LEAVES, STEM, ROOT

WILD LEEKS
LEAVES, STEM, ROOT

PURSLANE
LEAVES, STEM, SEEDS

Some wild plants taste better if you prepare them. For example, boiling purslane leaves may make them taste less sour. Check your plant identification guide before eating.

STAY AWAY!

Only eat wild plants if you're absolutely sure they're safe to eat. Eating the wrong thing could kill you. Many wild plants are poisonous. Some hurt you just by touching them, such as poison ivy. Some can kill you if you eat them, such as rhododendrons or nightshade.

Don't be fooled by food that seems safe. You may eat berries at home, but wild berries can make you very sick. And, whatever you do, *do not* eat mushrooms. Some kinds are the most harmful living **organisms** out there.

SURVIVAL TIP

A common saying is "Leaves of three, let it be." This means to stay away from plants with leaves in groups of three, such as poison ivy.

Identifying poisonous plants is as important a survival skill as identifying edible plants. Queen Anne's lace (below) is edible, but looks much like poison hemlock (top), which is deadly.

HUNTING AND TRAPPING

In survival **situations**, wild animals are a great source of food. Meat contains a lot of **protein** and fat, which give our bodies energy. Small game, such as squirrels, rabbits, and birds, are good animals to hunt.

Hunting takes practice and skill. Look for animal tracks to see if there's game in the area. Stay quiet and keep out of sight so you don't scare it away. Once you've caught your food, make sure to clean and cook it. Cooking it over a fire will make it safe to eat.

SURVIVAL TIP

If you've never used hunting weapons, hunting won't be a good option for finding food in the wilderness. Talk to a parent or guardian if you are interested in learning how to hunt.

Hunters use many kinds of tools and traps. These objects can be very dangerous. Never use hunting tools or traps without a parent or adult present.

17

EATING BUGS

Does the idea of eating bugs gross you out? If you're looking for food in the wilderness, you may have no other choice. Bugs are a great source of protein, and thousands of kinds are safe to eat.

Crickets and grasshoppers are common edible bugs. You can also eat many kinds of ants, beetles, centipedes, and mealworms. Look for bugs on leaves and under logs. Edible bugs are safe to eat raw or cooked. Some people think bugs are best when they're crunchy!

SURVIVAL TIP

Most bugs are safe to eat, but some can be poisonous. Stay away from spiders, bugs that smell bad, and bugs that are red, yellow, or orange.

Eating bugs isn't as weird as you might think. About 80 percent of the world's population eats bugs as part of an everyday diet!

LOVING OUR PLANET

The wilderness is full of wild food for people to eat, and it's there for our taking—so long as we understand and respect it. Wild plants are a good source of food, but picking too much can harm the plant population. Some plants take years to grow back, so only take what you need to eat.

Overhunting small game can upset nature's balance, too. Only hunt what you know you'll use. Finally, don't leave trash or waste in the woods. Keep nature clean for everyone to enjoy!

Keeping the wilderness clean makes it enjoyable for everyone.

STUDY UP

Although you won't use your survival skills every time you go into the wilderness, it's important to have them when you need them. You may not have to eat bugs during a simple camping trip, but you never know what can happen.

Spend time studying and using your survival skills, even when you're not in the wild. Read up on plants, look for bugs, and get to know your surroundings. If you ever find yourself needing food in the wilderness, you'll be happy you did!

GLOSSARY

description: Something that's written or spoken to tell what a person, object, or event is like.

energy: The power to do work.

identification: The action of telling who or what something is.

organism: A living thing, such as a plant or animal.

protein: Matter found in foods that is an important part of the human diet.

refuel: To eat in order to gain more energy.

shelter: A place that keeps a person safe from bad weather.

situation: A series of events in which a person finds himself or herself.

wilderness: A natural, wild place.

INDEX

WEBSITES

Due to the changing nature of Internet links, PowerKids Press has developed an online list of websites related to the subject of this book. This site is updated regularly. Please use this link to access the list: www.powerkidslinks.com/wss/food